AF271044

Praise for *Get Along, Get Ahead: 101 Courtesies for the New Workplace*

"Karen Hinds demonstrates how courtesy can lead to charisma, and politeness to productivity. This is a rare book that propels the reader forward by going back to good manners." **Alan Weiss, Ph.D., author of** *Million Dollar Consulting.*

"An engaging new book that illustrates how common courtesies are still essential in today's complex marketplace. *Get Along, Get Ahead* is a great primer for learning good business manners. **Marjorie Brody, MA, CSP, CMC, motivational speaker and author of** *Professional Impressions: Etiquette for Everyone Everyday.*

"Finally, there is a book that simply and concisely states what should be obvious rules of everyday conduct for civilized people. It's sad but true, that in today's chaotic work

world, such a book is needed and necessary."
Bruce L. Katcher, Ph.D., President, The Discovery Group.

"This book is for everyone who wants to make a positive impression while climbing the corporate ladder of success. It's packed with useful information that will help the busy business person become more polished, credible, and professional."
Carole Copeland-Thomas, MBA, Keynote Speaker and President of C. Thomas and Associates.

"Karen Hinds is right on target! This book covers all the basics and then some."
Rhonda F. Waters, Ph.D., President, The Mutare Group, Inc.

Get Along Get Ahead

101 Courtesies
for the
New Workplace

Karen S. Hinds

New Books Publishing
Boston, Massachusetts

New Books Publishing
Boston, Massachusetts

Hinds, Karen S.
Get Along, Get Ahead: 101 Courtesies for the New Workplace

ISBN 0-9679861-0-9

Library of Congress Card Number: 00-104773

DEDICATION

To my husband, Shugas D. Hinds, Sr., for his love and support; to my parents, Eustace and Rosita Edwards, who taught me how to dream; to my brothers and sisters, Jeffrey, Diana, Gaynelle, Rafique, and Raphael who listened to my crazy dreams. To my son, Shugas D. Hinds, Jr., for all the baby smiles that brighten my days.

ACKNOWLEDGMENTS

Thank you to the people who have supported me: Carol Pyne for your opinions, honesty, encouragement, and prayers; Noel Johnson for your guidance and inspiration; Carole Copeland-Thomas because you saw the flame in me and gave me a match to keep the fire lit; Snowden McFall for opening my eyes to new possibilities; Alecia Wilson, Judith Pineda-Edwards, Robert Felder, Christine Copeland, Arlene Lowney, Jim Ritscher, Laura Moore, Lurie Davis, Stephanie Heiter, NESA Mentee Group, Rick Segel, Darren LaCroix, Wayne Gignac, John Kremer, Sam Horn, Raymond E. Cole for your time and talent; and to The Rev. Dr. T. Anne Daniel for your prayers.

Cover Design: Culpdesign
    104 West Street
    East Bridgewater, Massachusetts 02333
    Culpdesign@aol.com

TABLE OF CONTENTS

FOREWORD

Snowden McFall *"The Fired Up! Motivator."*

Why Does Courtesy Matter in Today's FAST-PACED World?

In today's high technology world of e-mails and Web sites and fast, fast, fast Internet connections, it is easy to forget that the reason for all this technology and speed is to improve the quality of human lives. All too often, small courtesies and acts of kindness are forgotten or overlooked; people just don't seem to matter as much anymore.

And yet, for those of us who work with small or large businesses, we realize that politeness, kindness, and manners are sometimes the most important ways to form bonds with others. Taking the time to say please and thank you, including warm salutations at the beginning and end of e-mails, sharing a genuine smile with a check-out clerk: all of these are tiny

gestures that make a BIG difference in the
quality of our professional and
personal relationships.

*Manners Seem Absent From Much of
Today's Youth*

As a former educator of junior high school
children, I am frequently appalled at the lack
of manners exhibited by our youth today. The
courtesies and politeness that characterized
our classrooms 20 years ago seem long gone.
Our youth are not to blame, for these are the
values that have been passed on by
their parents.

Having grown up in the South, I did find the
various behaviors required of being a "lady"
somewhat burdensome. At the time, I didn't
understand the value of manners and
courtesy. But I do now. These simple
gestures are doorways to underlying kindness
and compassion that is so desperately needed
in this world. A callous disregard of the
dignity of other human beings is what enables
dictators to get away with torture and

genocide. Simply acknowledging the act of kindness between humans can mean the difference between life and death.

Small Courtesies Can Save Lives

Antione de Saint Exupery, the celebrated author of "The Little Prince" and many other books, told a story called "The Smile" about his days in prison when he was captured as a fighter pilot. Most of the time, his jailer ignored him and treated him with disdain. But at one point, when Saint Exupery asked for a match, the prison guard looked up at his prisoner. At that moment, Saint Exupery smiled at the guard, and something intangible, and yet deeply powerful took place. They began talking about their children and shared pictures with each other. They connected as human beings who had things in common. And later, as the time neared to take Saint Exupery to his death, his jailer instead unlocked the jail cell and led Exupery to freedom. All because of a smile.

A Unique Perspective

Karen Hinds, brings a unique perspective to her work. Born and raised in St. Vincent in the Caribbean, Karen grew up in a culture where manners and politeness are not only expected, they are mandatory. You need only visit a Caribbean country to see how much this is true. People are genuinely warm and friendly, and unerringly polite. It is one of the many things I love about that part of the world, and Karen's background gives her a perfect perspective on how different things are today in America.

Like myself, Karen worked first with youth and then adults as a teacher, and then professional speaker and author. We both have seen many of the same trends, and we know that rudeness is costing American businesses thousands of dollars each year. Rudeness leads to workplace unrest, and then to violence. It contributes to employment dissatisfaction, low employee retention, and even road rage. As violence is on the rise in so many places, one very easy solution is to go

back to the values of common courtesy
and kindness.

A Roadmap for the Future

In this book, *Get Along, Get Ahead: 101
Courtesies for the New Workplace*, Karen has
provided a roadmap for employees and
employers at all levels. Her common sense
approach is easy to follow and easy to use.
Her examples are straightforward and even
the most junior of employees should be able to
put these tools into practice immediately.

Managers and employers will find the
suggestions for how to defuse anger, deliver
feedback, and give credit especially useful.
Karen's strategies for successful workplace
courtesy include tips on body language, vocal
tone, and active listening. Her "Thanks A
Lot" chapter gives you concrete tools to
improve employee morale and retention.
"How Rude!" offers sound, step-by-step
advice for listening and defusing customer
frustrations and honoring their concerns.

With its comprehensive approach to modern business, and sound strategies for success Karen Hinds has provided an invaluable tool for any professional. I highly recommend this book to anyone in the workplace. I know I intend to keep my copy nearby on my desk, for quick and easy reference.

*Snowden McFall, "The Fired Up! Motivator," is a professional speaker and expert on business success strategies, and President and Owner of Brightwork Advertising and Training in Nashua,
New Hampshire.*

Web site: www.firedup-takeaction-now.com
Web site: www.brightworkadvertising.com

INTRODUCTION

This is a book for employees. You may still be in or fresh out of school, starting your first job, changing jobs or careers, or moving to a new position with the same employer. You may work on the line, in the shop, or administrative pool or you may have managerial or sales responsibilities. Whatever your situation, common courtesies are the foundation of success in the workplace.

Throughout your work life, you will have relationships with three groups of people: coworkers, customers, and supervisors/ managers. You must learn to handle all three of these relationships. Just knowing what to do, having the skills or experience to get the job done, is not enough in these times.

Read this book because:

- You want to be successful in your present job.

- You want to be ready when the
  opportunity to move on comes along.

- Like you, your coworkers want to
  feel good coming to work each day.

- Your boss knows that amicable
  employee relationships contribute to
  the profit margin of the company.

- Your boss knows, and you should
  too, that satisfied customers become
  repeat customers who grow
  the business.

This book offers you an easy to read collection
of courtesies that many employees never think
of, especially in the early days on the job
when new relationships are being established.
The first three chapters focus on courtesy with
coworkers, customers, and your supervisor/
manager. The next chapter covers courtesy
from managers to employees. Chapter five
revisits basic courtesies. A bonus chapter
follows on courtesy in the technological age.

There are additional resources in the appendix on networking skills and building a more professional image. There is also an interesting list of duties expected of employees back in 1872!

May you find and give respect and courtesy in your workplace and create for yourself a successful and satisfying work life!

WHY IS WORKPLACE COURTESY SO IMPORTANT?

Our society is experiencing an increase in violence and incivility in homes, schools, and on the road. This is also seeping into the workplace and causing business leaders to sit up and take notice.

An insulting boss, a coworker who yells or torments other workers, crude jokes at the expense of others, arriving late for work, tardiness to meetings, unhelpful people on the phone, or absentminded store clerks are but a few of the rude and discourteous behaviors people encounter daily. It's these day-to-day habits and behaviors that can bleed an organization dry of its talent, its morale, and its loyal customers; hinder efficient production; and hamper the company's ability to compete in the marketplace.

Supervisors/managers understand that they must pay attention to the little things. In other words, behavior that is disrespectful,

inconsiderate, and selfish cannot go
unchallenged if the firm seeks to realize its full
potential. What was overlooked or put
up with a few years ago will not be
tolerated today.

Customers are also unwilling to accept rude
behavior. Technological advances have
created more options for customers when
deciding with whom to build a business
relationship. They can easily switch to a
competitor where the focus is on building
solid relationships and they feel the service
is better.

This book shares with you the habits and
behaviors that will increase courtesy and
civility in your workplace and enhance your
chances for success in your chosen work.

"Manners easily and rapidly mature
into morals."
Horace Mann

"Etiquette is getting sleepy in company
and not showing it."
Hyman Maxwell Berston

"You can get through life with bad
manners, but it's easier with
good manners."
Lillian Gish

"Manners are like the zero in the
arithmetic; they may not be much in
themselves, but they are capable of
adding a great deal to the value of
everything else."
Freya Stark

CHAPTER ONE

Courtesy with Coworkers

- Thanks A Lot

- Blowing Off Steam Before
  You Blow Your Top

- Have You Got
  Some Attitude!

- No More Traffic Jams

- We've Got to Start
  Meeting Like This

THANKS A LOT

Though simple, showing your appreciation
can have the most positively amazing effects.
People are burned out on bad news and
insensitive attitudes. Letting individuals
know they are valued is a sure way of
cementing business and personal relationships
and building new ones.

*"Appreciation is like an insurance policy. It has to
be renewed every now and then."*
Dave McIntyre.

1

Always say "thank you."

Say "thank you" when others help or complete projects and tasks. This shows your appreciation for the work being done.

"The worst mistake a boss can make is not to say 'well done.'" John Ashcroft

2

Always say "please" when asking someone to perform a task.

Even though you are all being paid, saying please demonstrates that you also respect each one as an individual.

"Great spirits have always encountered violent opposition from mediocre minds." Albert Einstein

3

Greet everyone.
Say "Good Morning" or "Good Evening" with
a genuine smile to people you may take for
granted such as the parking lot attendant,
your assistant, the building maintenance
person, etc. This builds relationships and
shows everyone that they are valued
and respected regardless of status.

4

Compliment someone every day.
The power of a compliment is often
overlooked. Try it, and understand its power.

*"I have yet to be bored by someone paying me a
compliment."* Otto Van Isch.

5

Do something nice for someone.
Acts of genuine kindness are guaranteed to keep everyone refreshed and excited about the task at hand.

"No act of kindness, no matter how small, is ever wasted." Aesop

6

Send thank you cards in a timely fashion.
Ideally within one week when gifts are received, when someone does something for you, or after attending a special event.

"One of life's gifts is that each of us, no matter how tired and downtrodden, finds reasons for thankfulness."
J. Robert Moskin

BLOWING OFF STEAM BEFORE YOU BLOW YOUR TOP

The dramatic increase in violence in our schools, homes, streets, and workplaces has proven time after time that we have become a society that has forgotten the rules of self-discipline and self-control.

Reversing this disturbing trend begins with the individual, long before anger and dissatisfaction balloon into rage. It is consciously choosing to be in control of your emotions and decisions rather than consciously choosing to be out of control, impolite, or even abusive.

"Anyone can become angry. That is easy. But to be angry with the right person, to the right degree, at the right time, for the right purpose, and in the right way – that is not easy."   Aristotle

7

Tell the truth.

There is no difference between a "white lie" used to escape uncomfortable situations or a "real lie." They both involve using deception and manipulation and those techniques are always unacceptable.

"To be persuasive, we must be believable. To be believable, we must be credible. To be credible we must tell the truth."
Edward R. Murrow

8

Do not interrupt.

Let others voice their opinions and finish their sentences, then respond.

"The wit of conversation consists more in finding it in others than in showing a great deal yourself."
Jean De La Bruyere

9

Apologize when you make a mistake.

Do what is right in spite of what your ego, your pride, and office politics may dictate.

"Always do right. This will gratify some people, and astonish the rest." Mark Twain

10

Pick your battles carefully and avoid angry outbursts.

When faced with a potentially angry situation, train yourself to stop and think. Is it really worth it? With road rage, school yard rage, and air rage no one needs your outrage.

"When a man angers you, he conquers you."
Toni Morrison

11

All gossip is bad gossip.

You promote gossip when you start it, repeat it, or listen to it. Excuse yourself or politely change the topic.

"Live so that people who know you will not believe the gossip about you." Anonymous

12

Do not insult or embarrass people publicly.

Ask to speak to the person in private before the situation escalates, and after you're in control of your emotions. Remind yourself that your insults are really a reflection of your inability to exercise self-control and diplomacy.

"Do not use a hatchet to remove a fly from your friend's forehead." *Chinese Proverb*

13

Deliver feedback/criticism in a healthy, constructive manner.

Abusive e-mails, memos, phone messages, and confrontations will never shape a mediocre worker into an exemplary worker. Verbal abuse kills the spirit and dries up creativity.

"Sandwich every bit of criticism between two layers of praise." Mary Kay Ash

14

Be mindful of your language.

There is no justification for the use of foul, coarse, blunt, abusive, or derogatory statements. Avoid terms of endearment such as "dear," "hon," "doll," and the like as they, too, can be demeaning.

"The limits of my language means the limits of my world." Ludwig Wittgenstein

15

Give credit where credit is due.

Recognizing someone for work done can improve interpersonal relationships, increase output, and boost overall employee morale, all of which ultimately affect the bottom line.

"Credit is something that should be given to others. If you are in a position to give credit to yourself, then you do not need it."
Hollywood Character Monroe Stahr

16

Offer solutions, not criticism.

Face the challenge of finding solutions. Conduct a brainstorming session, assess the options, and/or ask others for help. Placing blame, though easy, is counter productive.

"Problems are only opportunities in work clothes."
Henry Kissinger

17

Treat all people as you would like to be treated.

Whether you're interacting with the CEO or the janitor, stop and visualize yourself in the other person's position. What would you want to hear, feel, think, or even remember? Then do everything in your power to give him/her that experience.

"When we put ourselves in other people's shoes, we're less likely to want to put them in their place." Farmer's Digest

18

Crude jokes are never funny.

Sent via the Internet or told at gatherings, jokes that discriminate or make fun of any group are offensive and can be grounds for lawsuits.

"The only weapon that becomes sharper with constant use is the tongue." Anonymous

19

Listen more, talk less.
Listen to what is said and what is not. You
will see people and situations in a new light
and make better decisions.

*"Wisdom is the reward you get for a lifetime of
listening when you'd have preferred to talk."*
Doug Larson

20

Listen with your whole body.
Give eye contact, respond with nods and
affirmative words, don't jump to conclusions,
paraphrase to make sure you understand.

"People ought to listen more slowly."
Jean Sparks Ducey

21

When unclear, ask questions.

What you say and what the listener hears can be very different. Ask, "Did I hear you correctly?" then repeat what you understood.

"It is better to debate a question without settling it than to settle a question without debating it."
Joseph Joubert.

22

Be patient with people who have limited command of English.

More than ever immigrants are stepping in to fill the many vacant positions in the job market. They add value as coworkers, customers, and business partners and deserve the same respect as a proficient speaker.

"Patience is the ability to put up with people you'd like to put down." Ulrike Ruffert

23

Refrain from speaking in a secretive manner while in the company of others.
Excuse yourself from the group for private conversations to avoid creating an atmosphere of exclusion and distrust.

"While all deception requires secrecy, all secrecy is not meant to deceive."
Frank Trippet

24

Maintain eye contact when talking.
It says that you are confident, attentive to others, and care about what they are saying.

"The eyes are the window to the soul."

HAVE YOU GOT SOME ATTITUDE!

Practicing courtesy begins with your mental attitude every moment of the day and the decisions you make about how to act or react in any given situation. It takes strength and courage to maintain a positive attitude, look for the good in all circumstances, or find the lessons to be learned when faced with difficult or uncomfortable events. You will need discipline and perseverance.

"Attitude… will make or break a company… a church… a home…. We have a choice everyday regarding the attitude we will embrace for that day."
Charles Swindoll.

25

Renew your attitude daily.

It's difficult to work with or serve bitter, unhappy people. Take time everyday to mentally map a positive day. Create your day with positive thoughts and ideas and meditate on them moment to moment.

"As a man thinketh in his heart, so is he."
Proverbs 23:7

26

Be even tempered.

Deadlines, errors, and pressure to produce can be stressful. Be self-controlled, avoid frequent or extreme mood swings.

"Education is the ability to listen to almost anything without losing your temper or your self-confidence." Robert Frost

27

Smile!

Create a warm and inviting atmosphere that will build excellent rapport with customers and coworkers.

"Think excitement, talk excitement, and you are bound to be an excited person."
Norman Vincent Peale

28

Be aware of your tone of voice.

Avoid sarcastic and condescending tones when addressing coworkers, customers, and management. Pay attention to your feelings as they often dictate your tone of voice.

"It's not what you say, but how you say it."

29

Clean up your own mess.

Eliminate the need for signs all over the break
room appliances. These are a convenience
not a right.

NO MORE TRAFFIC JAMS

Telecommuting has existed for as long as there have been traveling sales people. However, over the past 10 years the number of people working from home has increased.

To stay competitive in the current labor market, more employers are offering telecommuting as an option to current and incoming employees as one way to retain and attract excellent employees.

Technologically enabled employees can spend more time at home with their families while still meeting their employers' needs and producing the agreed upon results.

"When thou enter a city, abide by its customs."
The Talmud

30

Limit personal use of company property.

The equipment is for company business and not for your part-time job or starting your company or other personal uses. Integrity must be maintained at all times.

31

Expect 24 hours notice for visits.

Home visits are not the norm, but if needed, request 24 hours notice, as it is a private home.

32

Report for all necessary meetings.

Telecommuters are not exempt from company meetings and must attend when the request is made.

33

Inform coworkers of your schedule.

Planning meetings, conference calls, and contacting you will be easier when the office knows the days and hours you work.   If possible put your calendar on the Web.

34

Minimize background noise.

Quiet the kids, the pets, the TV, and other noises that may be distracting, especially while on the telephone. You may be working at home yet professionalism is still expected.

35

Maintain contact with your office on a regular basis.

Stay in touch with the office through e-mail, voice mail, a person to person conversation, audio conference and/or video conference calls. Keeping informed about developments in the office and informing others of your progress is still expected.

WE'VE GOT TO START MEETING LIKE THIS

In some organizations, the word meeting is synonymous with headaches. Although necessary, too many meetings are often misused and or mismanaged.

Since time is of the essence in this part of the western hemisphere, simple courtesies can be employed to make meetings and the general use of time efficient and productive.

"I have only just a minute
Only sixty seconds in it,
Forced upon me — can't refuse it.
Didn't seek it, didn't choose it.
I must suffer if I lose it.
Give account if I abuse it.
Just a tiny little minute
But eternity is in it."

Benjamin E. Mays

36

RSVP by the date requested.

This helps the host or meeting planner accurately meet all the needs of the occasion to ensure its success.

37

Arrive on time.

By the time your day or meeting is scheduled to begin, you should have completed your refreshment run (coffee, bagel) and actual work should start at the appointed time. The best way to accomplish this is to arrive 5-10 minutes early, which eliminates the misuse of company time.

38

Be prepared for all meetings and appointments.

It shows that you are committed, and it saves time and money.

39

Stick to the agenda.

It's best to review the agenda before the meeting. You will know the purpose and can come prepared to contribute.

40

Respect the facilitator.

An effective facilitator minimizes time spent on unrelated topics, keeps the meeting on purpose, helps delegate tasks, ensures all opinions are heard, and focuses the meeting on achieving results.

41

Stay awake during meetings and presentations.

Maintain your professionalism at all times even though some meetings are more interesting than others. Drink a little coffee or cold water to stay awake.

42

Make the most of break times.

The attention span of the average person is short. For maximum participation in meetings, take care of your needs during the breaks (walk, stretch, feet up, etc.).

43

Leave only when meeting ends.

It's rude, unprofessional, and disruptive to walk out. Notify the host/presenter before the meeting begins if you must leave early.

CHAPTER TWO

Courtesy with Customers

- **More Than You Could Hope For**

- **How Rude!**

MORE THAN YOU COULD HOPE FOR

Although massive customer solicitation campaigns can bring in new customers, time and effort are better spent on improving the level of service that is being offered to current customers and retaining their loyalty.

Studies show that it takes 5 times the resources to find a new customer than it does to keep the one already doing business with the company. Once a reputation for excellent service is established, customers will naturally gravitate to it.

"The customer may not always be right, but he/she is the one with the money." Anonymous

44

Greet customers immediately.

Give a verbal greeting, acknowledge them with body language if busy (smile, hand signal) then offer your service promptly.

45

Follow-up with customers.

Call, send a note, or an e-mail. This shows that the service being provided does not stop until the customer's needs are exceeded.

46

Be attentive.

Give each customer your undivided attention whether on the phone or in person. The customer being served is the most important person at that time.

47

Anticipate the customer's needs.

Figure out and provide what customers need before they know they need it.

48

Practice flexibility.

Customers like to know that you can work with and meet their demands on a timely basis. This may mean going the extra mile to keep them happy.

49

Thank customers for
their business.

At the end of calls, always say "thank you"or when appropriate send a card or note. Let your clients know that they are appreciated.

HOW RUDE!

Difficult customers are people with unmet needs. The job of a customer service representative is to turn the situation around and do what is necessary to meet those needs and make that customer happy.

Complaining customers are basically trying to communicate that there is something about the way the organization conducts its business that does not work for them. It usually will take extra effort to investigate and resolve complaints.

"We should never be allowed to forget that it is the customer who, in the end, determines how many people are employed and what sort of wages companies can afford." Lord Robbens

50

Give them answers.
Tell them how their problem will be fixed.
Give them the options available to resolve
their complaints immediately.

51

**Remain calm when dealing with
angry customers.**
Count to ten, take a deep breath, or
delegate the task. Customers refer to the
company as "you." Try not to take
this personally.

52

**Listen to and empathize with
unhappy customers.**
Customers are your business. They want to
know that their opinions and suggestions are
being taken seriously.

53

Know your chain of command when transferring customers.

Direct the call or person to a supervisor, another colleague, or department. Customers become more upset when bounced around to unhelpful, non-decision makers or are barred from accessing decision makers.

54

Be available, take your time.

Customers like to know that a representative is on hand to meet their requirements when needed.

55

Apologize for inconveniences.

Sometimes an apology is all a customer needs. Go the extra mile to ensure they continue to patronize your establishment.

CHAPTER THREE

Courtesy from Employees to Managers

- **Moving On Up:**
  The Empowered Employee

MOVING ON UP:
THE EMPOWERED EMPLOYEE

Because the workplace has undergone many different changes in the last ten years, successful employees today need to embrace new values and operate differently if they are to remain an invaluable asset to their employer.

"The one who adapts his policy to the times prospers, and likewise the one whose policy clashes with the demands of the times does not."
Niccolo Machiavelli

56

Call ahead when plans change.
Call the appropriate person if unable to keep an appointment, report for work, or when running late. Your absence may impact other people's schedules and decision making abilities. Prompt notice is needed to make other plans.

57

Minimize non-work interruptions.
Make better use of time by limiting social visits from coworkers. Close your door and/or hang a creative "Do Not Disturb" sign on your desk or cubicle.

58

Be coachable.
Change in today's work world is a given. Being open to new ideas and stepping out of your comfort zone will ensure a path to success.

59

Promptly notify the manager when machines do not work.
Time is wasted when problems are not reported immediately and taken care of. Ignoring damaged/jammed equipment (fax, copy machine, shredder, etc.) slows down workflow and production.

60

Do not use office mates as your personal psychologist.
Time spent listening to the personal concerns of coworkers or telling one's personal problems equals lost production.

61

Manage up.

Employers are now seeking independent thinkers, workers with an entrepreneurial spirit yet able to follow the vision of the leadership, a team player, and employees who can meet the needs of their supervisor by staying one step ahead.

62

Think results.

Results keep companies in business and it is imperative that employees understand this fact and strive to meet deadlines without sacrificing quality.

63

Get the big picture.

Learn all you can about how your daily tasks affect the company as a whole. Be aware and understand the entire process as well as your particular job.

64

Be knowledgeable about the product or service you are providing.

All employees need to be in a constant state of learning. Being the best means knowing all aspects of the product or service being offered. This sets the stage for exceptional service.

CHAPTER FOUR

Courtesy from Managers to Employees

- We Really Value Our Employees
- Different Strokes for Different Folks
- We Believe in You
- It Starts at the Top

WE REALLY VALUE OUR EMPLOYEES

Strong, effective, empowered employees are the ones who are treated with respect and dignity and have access to the knowledge, resources, and skills needed to perform their jobs.

Companies are trying creative means to reward and retain their employees such as special stock options, international day trips, to a day at the beach. First, however, creative managers need to utilize the skills necessary to understand, motivate, and create an environment conducive to exceptional performance.

Managers need to know how to work with a diverse workforce. There is a significant increase in the number of baby boomers, generation Xers, women, immigrants, and people of color who are entering the workforce for the first time or are reentering.

According to the Hudson Institute's Workforce 2000 report, 85% of new entrants to the workforce will be in the latter three of the above list from the year 2000 onward.

"A good manager is a man [or woman] who isn't worried about his [or her] career but rather the careers of those who work for him [or her]."
HSM Burns

"It is the responsibility of the leadership and the management to give opportunities and put demands on people which enable them to grow as human beings in the work environment."
Sir John Harvey-Jones

65

Lead by example.

Employees respond more to a coaching style than an authoritative style since it demonstrates that they are valued and can make a contribution in achieving the goals at hand. As a coach, working in the trenches is important to building an empowered team.

"Great opportunities to help others seldom come, but small ones surround us everyday."
Sally Koch

66

Admit it when you make an error.

Employees are sometimes blamed for mistakes even when it's not justified. Empowered managers know that in the pursuit of perfection, mistakes will be made. Seeing mistakes as lessons to be learned and taking ownership of them is part of the process.

"To conduct great matters and never commit a fault is above the force of human nature." Plutarch

67

**Give clear concise directions
and requests.**
Candid and honest communication is now
expected. Errors often occur when employees
are unsure of the request being made.
Encourage them to ask questions if they are
not clear.

68

**Avoid public discussions of any
confidential employee matters.**
Whether it's with other managers, friends, or
coworkers it is inappropriate, unprofessional,
and undermines the trust your
position carries.

*"Discretion is being able to raise your eyebrow
instead of your voice."* Anon

69

Provide the necessary tools and information in a timely fashion to successfully execute daily tasks.
To maximize the effectiveness of employees, consistent training must be available
and utilized.

"Training is everything. The peach was once a bitter almond; cauliflower is nothing but a cabbage with a college education." Mark Twain

70

Build in room for on-the-job creativity.
Today's workers like to know they add value
and that the responsibilities they hold
are substantive.

"Never tell people how to do things. Tell them what to do and they will surprise you with their ingenuity." General George S. Patton, Jr.

71

**Learn from any
knowledgeable employee.**
Consider the value of the information needed
and not the age, race, gender, or position of
the person who has it.

*"Knowledge is like a garden: if it is not
cultivated it cannot be harvested."*
Guinea Proverb.

DIFFERENT STROKES
FOR DIFFERENT FOLKS

Understanding and working with diverse populations is a given for any company to be competitive in the 21st century.
Understanding the new diversity is knowing it encompasses more than race.

"Prejudice is the child of ignorance."
William Hazlitt

"It is not best that we all should think alike, it is differences of opinion that make horse races."
Mark Twain

72

Create an environment that celebrates differences.

Let your personnel be a reflection of the global community along ethnic, gender, personal beliefs, and generational lines. Encourage programs and activities that support these differences.

A diverse work place ensures that there will always be an abundance of fresh perspectives, and it provides the means for understanding and meeting the needs of all customers.

73

Be aware of intergenerational dynamics.

Respect does not require an age criteria as generation Xers and baby boomers meet in the workplace.

74

Be patient with technologically challenged workers.

Generation X employees tend to be more computer literate. Use that knowledge to bridge generational gaps instead of building dividers.

#75

Treat all employees fairly.

Favoritism and/or double standards along gender, racial, or social lines can undermine the soul of your organization and produce a hostile work environment.

WE BELIEVE IN YOU

Effective managers know that in order to get the most and the best quality work from staff, support systems and motivational breaks must be utilized to keep the workforce in top shape.

"Call it what you will, incentives are what get people to work harder." Nikita Khruschev

"No man is an island unto himself. Each is a piece of the continent, a part of the main." John Donne

76

Offer consistent support to employees.
Listen to opinions, take seriously any suggestions to improve work flow and processes, then act on the information gathered.

77

Practice family friendly management.
Employees are striving more towards balancing family and work life. Making provisions for employees to take care of sick children, school activities, or an elderly parent is critical to high employee retention.

78

Allow your employees to share the spotlight.
Great feats are always accomplished through team efforts.

79

Creatively reward, encourage, and motivate your employees.

Use humor, ongoing activities, games, and food experiences, or get involved with community projects. Offer a signing bonus, stock options, referral bonus, flex time, adventure outings, concierge services, or discounts on services.

80

Publicly acknowledge employees.

Employees who go above and beyond on a regular basis need to be recognized for their extra efforts.

81

Give name recognition.

Reassure employees that ALL efforts are important. Use announcements at team meetings, company gatherings, or the newsletter as a means of recognition.

IT STARTS AT THE TOP

Courtesy has been regarded as an individual responsibility and was not typically associated with organizations. However, the tight labor market has forced companies to look at the image they project and be very conscious about how they treat employees. Employee friendly policies and practices are no longer an option, but a necessity to retain and attract every potential worker, not just top talent. Managers who have influence over company policy need to exercise that influence in shaping the organization.

"When people go to work, they shouldn't have to leave their hearts at home."
Betty Bender

82

Notify unsuccessful job applicants after interviews.

It reflects badly on a company's image if, after an interview, applicants are told they will be contacted and then do not receive any correspondence. Send an e-mail, make a phone call, send a card.

83

Encourage the use of benefits.

These are outlined in the company handbook. Flextime, telecommuting, and parental leaves should be clearly explained and promoted. Educate workers, create the right processes, and hire the staff needed to ensure benefit programs work without too much stress.

84

Create an environment of trust.

Take time to build and practice effective communication skills, speak openly, and avoid double talk.

85

Provide a way to obtain feedback from employees.

Set up a complaint hotline, suggestion box, or Web site for employees to voice concerns and then act on them. Consider an ombudsperson.

86

Deal with employee complaints and concerns promptly.

Ensure employees are safe, satisfied, confident, and productive to clear roadblocks to quality production.

87

Address problem employees early.

Side stepping or ignoring a problem gives the impression that the behavior is condoned, and that can adversely affect excellent employees.

88

Handle dismissals professionally.

Secretive or public dismissals are problematic. Advise employees of staff changes and do not feed the office grapevine.

CHAPTER FIVE

Basic Courtesy Revisited

- That Ought to be
  Common Sense

- It's How They See It

THAT OUGHT TO BE
COMMON SENSE

Even though the workplace is changing, the old rules still apply. These basic rules should be the foundation of courteous behavior as we interact with others each day.

"There is always a best way of doing everything, if it be to boil an egg. Manners are the happy ways of doing things." Emerson

89

**Don't yell across the office or
at coworkers.**

It's disruptive, distracting, and inappropriate.

90

Eavesdropping is never acceptable.

You're admitting by your actions that you're
invading someone else's privacy and usually
the information being discussed doesn't
directly concern you.

91

Promptly return borrowed items.

Borrowing means you are allowed
temporary use of an item. Return the item
and obtain your own.

92

Notify the appropriate person if you used the last item from the supply closet.

Minimize undue stress caused by the lack of small items like fax toner, ink cartridges, writing pads, and other supplies.

93

Respect individual property.

Do not rummage through desks or rearrange absent employees' space. It's an invasion of their personal space and utterly disrespectful.

94

Keep your space organized.

Keep files and databases tidy and orderly as this will help coworkers to step in on your behalf in an emergency.

95

Reserve the office conference room ahead of time.

If you are in someone else's time block, quietly leave when asked to. Do not pull rank. Negotiate ahead of time if the spot you need is taken.

96

Avoid reading over other people's shoulders.

This is an invasion of personal space (approximately 2 ft. around).

97

Don't pressure coworkers to buy your child's school candy, tickets, etc.

Yes, your child wants to win the top prize but coworkers can feel depleted with solicitations throughout the year. Let the buying be voluntary.

IT'S HOW THEY SEE IT

It's not what you say it's how they see it. Make sure that your body language and what you say are in harmony. The body is a tell tale sign of how a person really feels.

"I know you believe you understand what you think I said, but I am not sure you realize that what you heard was not what I meant." Anonymous

98

Avoid negative body signals.

Crossed arms, sideways glances, frowning, biting fingernails, chewing pens or pencils, hissing, and pointing a finger are a few of the signs that indicate defensiveness, frustration, insecurity, or nervousness.

99

Practice positive body language.

Sit up tall, chin up, smile, hands behind your back when standing, steeple hands, and open hands are all signs of confidence, cooperation, and openness and should be perfected.

100

Cover your mouth.

After coughing or sneezing remember to clean that hand BEFORE offering it in a handshake. Use a wipe or wash up.

101

Give dry, firm handshakes.

Keep a tissue in your pocket or handbag and
discreetly dry hands before shaking,
if necessary.

BONUS
CHAPTER SIX

Courtesy with Technology

- ## Are You The Person To Whom I'm Speaking?

- ## Call Me on My Cell Phone

- ## It Takes Cooperation: Conference Calls

- ## Fax It

- ## Cybersurfing is Work

ARE YOU THE PERSON TO WHOM I'M SPEAKING?

The telephone sometimes seems like an extension of us, yet proper usage, especially in business settings, is still sorely lacking. The aim should be to make each phone conversation a pleasant, efficient, and productive experience for all parties involved.

"An invention of the devil, which abrogates some of the advantages of making a disagreeable person keep his distance."
Ambrose (Gwinett) Bierce

Bonus-1

Answer a phone by the third ring.

A quick response saves time for both parties
and clearly shows that the
organization is easily accessible to all.

Bonus-2

Speak cheerfully and clearly into the phone.

Your tone of voice should say you are ready to
exceed the needs of the customer on the other
end.

Bonus-3

Identify yourself when answering the phone.

"Hello, this is Janet, how may I help you?" or
"Hello, Customer Service, this is Janet, how
may I help you?" Callers will know that
they've reached the right person and
correct department.

Bonus-4

Return phone calls in 24 hours.

Competition is tight. Returning a call at your leisure can equal lost business. Technology ensures that we can no longer use the excuse "I was out of town," or "I was too busy."

Bonus-5

Avoid personal phone calls during work hours.

Use breaks instead of company time. Keep the conversation short if personal business must be conducted during office hours.

Bonus-6

Take accurate phone messages.

Print legibly or type messages, record who called, when, why, take a number, then deliver the message as soon as possible to the correct person.

Bonus-7

Speak slowly when leaving your number.

Repeat your contact information slowly to make it easier for the person retrieving the message. Your voice speed need not sound like an auctioneer.

Bonus-8

Ask to put someone on hold BEFORE you do.

Remember to go back and pick up the call within 30-40 seconds. Let callers know ahead of time if they may be on hold for more than 2 minutes. Check back periodically to ask if they would like to continue holding.

Bonus-9

Place calls on hold or hang up completely.

It's disastrous if the person on the line accidentally overhears you venting your frustration about the conversation you just had or speaking in a derogatory manner about him or her.

Bonus-10

Learn to transfer calls in the proper manner.

Dialing an extension without placing the call on hold is hard on the ears and forwarding calls to the wrong extension is annoying.

Bonus-11

Don't hang up the phone before someone is finished speaking.

Never hang up on a customer.

Bonus-12

Ask for permission before using a speaker phone.

Callers who are picked up on speakers may feel the person on the other end is preoccupied with other business.

CALL ME ON MY CELL PHONE

Cell phones have revolutionized the lives of every business person. It's easier and quicker to reach your desired party, but such conveniences can be hazardous while driving and disruptive to some aspects of everyday business operations.

"The real problem is not whether machines think, but whether men do."
B. F. Skinner

Bonus-13

Turn off cell phones and beepers.

The constant beeping and ringing from
different cell phones and beepers annoy
meeting attendees and ruin
recorded meetings.

Bonus-14

Use vibrate or flashing light features.

When expecting an urgent call during a
meeting, use these features to
minimize disturbances.

Bonus-15

Lower voice level when using phone in public.

The public does not need to hear the details of
your conversation.

IT TAKES COOPERATION: CONFERENCE CALLS
(Audio, Video, and Internet)

Bonus-16

Designate a call facilitator.

The facilitator is responsible for directing the conversation flow so everyone is able to make his or her point.

Bonus-17

Identify yourself each time you speak
(for audio).

Participants listening may not recognize your voice, so say who you are until they do.

Bonus-18

Wait your turn to speak.

It's the polite thing to do and it can be imperative if your audio equipment only transmits one speaker at a time.

Bonus-19

Maintain a quiet room.

Conference equipment can be very sensitive to background sounds so keep the noise to a minimum. Rustling papers, constant fidgeting with the furniture, noisy clothing, tapping, slurping drinks, or chewing food or gum loudly is a distraction.

Bonus-20

Stay within camera range.

Set up seating arrangements so visual contact is made with all speakers. People like to see who is talking.

FAX IT

The fax machine is a relatively recent addition to the host of communication equipment designed to speed up the communication process. When used correctly, efficiency can be improved, but too often important documents disappear, are never received, or are undeliverable.

"It has become appallingly obvious that our technology has exceeded our humanity."
Albert Einstein

Bonus-21

Distribute incoming faxes that are piled up at the machine.

Assign someone to this task and eliminate both the black hole that often consumes incoming faxes and the need to stand at the machine when you are expecting documents.

Bonus-22

Notify recipient when faxes are about to be sent.

Calling ahead will alert the receiver to check the machine for accuracy in transmission.

Bonus-23

Provide a cover sheet.

Include the sender's name and phone number, the recipient's name and phone number, and the number of pages being sent.

Bonus-24

Don't send private information.

The confidentiality statement on most cover sheets does not guarantee confidentiality. No one may admit it, but people do read other people's faxes.

CYBERSURFING IS WORK

The Internet isn't run by one organized system, but there are commonly accepted rules that govern this virtual highway. No tickets on this highway, but adhering to these rules projects a polished image and builds solid relationships with people you may never see or speak with, but who depend on your written words.

"The Internet is so big, so powerful and pointless that for some people it is a complete substitute for life." Andrew Brown

Bonus-25

Resist the urge to send frivolous e-mails, especially chain letters.

Companies are capable of monitoring all Internet usage. If you've been spammed, it is unwise to request removal from a mailing list. This just tells them it is a valid e-mail address. Ask your manager what the company "spam"policy is.

Bonus-26

Do not send e-mails typed in BOLD CAPITAL LETTERS.

This is the equivalent of yelling in cyberspace.

Bonus-27

Send complete e-mails.

Fill in the subject line, address the recipient by name and include your e-signature (name, department, company, and phone number).

Bonus-28

Check e-mail at least twice daily.

E-mail eliminates telephone tag and provides a fast, cost effective, and efficient way to correspond, so reply within 24-36 hours or sooner.

Bonus-29

Keep it simple.

Keep e-mail correspondence short. Messages need to be precise, but still adhere to the rules of business writing. Limit each e-mail to only one topic.

Bonus-30

Be selective when you CC.

Send carbon copies of e-mails only to those who will find the information useful. Remember to send the information only and delete all the forwarding addresses that sometimes come before.

APPENDIX

- Food Habits

- 10 Tips for Networking Success

- 10 Ways to Nurture a New Business Relationship

- Rules for Office Workers Back in 1872

- 12 Ways to Get Along and Get Ahead

- Workplace Statistics

- Suggested Reading List

FOOD HABITS

(a)

Your Mom was right, do not speak with food in your mouth.
The sight can be repulsive and hazardous to the person sitting across from you.

(b)

Eat only at meetings designated for meals or if refreshments are provided.
The aroma is often distracting and it is impolite.

(c)

Eat only what you placed in the shared office refrigerator.
Hungry people can be angry people especially when their homemade lunch is missing.

(d)

Refill the coffee pot.

If you drank the last cup or there are less than two cups remaining, your coworkers will appreciate it when you replenish it.

(e)

Avoid eating at your desk.

Food odors can be very distracting and long lasting; be considerate of your coworkers.

(f)

Never chew gum at work.

Gum is inappropriate, noisy, and rude.

10 TIPS FOR NETWORKING SUCCESS

1. Bring lots of business cards

2. Don't give more than one card unless asked

3. Ask politely for someone's card

4. Avoid the card collecting marathon

5. Address people by the name on the name tag

6. Be prepared to describe what you do in 30 seconds or less

7. Avoid discussing controversial topics

8. Get to know 3-5 people really well

9. Ask meaningful questions

10. Discuss work challenges, joys of the job, or mutual interests

10 WAYS
TO NURTURE A NEW CUSTOMER RELATIONSHIP

1. Follow up with a personal note, call, or e-mail after first meeting

2. If you promised to do something, do it ASAP

3. Send birthday and seasonal cards

4. Send helpful information (articles, tips, or e-mails) with a brief note

5. Ask for opinions on projects you might be working on

6. Invite the person to lunch

7. Refer prospects

8. Offer a subscription to your e-zine (don't sign them up without asking)

9. Send promotional materials when appropriate

10. Request feedback with a brief survey or questionnaire

RULES
FOR OFFICE WORKERS
BACK IN 1872

1. Office employees each day will fill lamps, clean chimneys, and trim wicks. Wash windows once a week.

2. Each clerk will bring in a bucket of water and a scuttle of coal for the day's business.

3. Make your pens carefully. You may whittle nibs to your individual taste.

4. Men employees will be given an evening off each week for courting purposes, or two evenings a week if they go regularly to church.

5. After thirteen hours of labor in the office, the employee should spend the remaining time reading the Bible and other good books.

6. Every employee should lay aside from each pay a goodly sum of his earnings for his

benefit during his declining years so that he
will not become a burden to society.

7. Any employee who smokes Spanish cigars,
uses liquor in any form, frequents pool and
public halls, or gets shaved in a barber shop
will give good reason to suspect his worth,
intentions, integrity, and honesty.

8. The employee who has performed his labor
faithfully and without fault for five years will
be given an increase of five cents in his pay,
providing profits from business permit it.

Anonymous
Boston Herald, 5 October 1958

12 WAYS TO GET ALONG AND GET AHEAD.

1. Be polite and respectful to everyone you come across regardless of income, title, race, gender, or difference of opinion.

2. Never intimidate other employees nor allow other employees to intimidate you.

3. Be eager to learn and willing to teach.

4. Be well groomed from head to toe and let your wardrobe say that business is still conducted even on casual Fridays.

5. Respect is earned, not demanded.

6. Look cheerful, have a ready smile for everyone, and never sulk.

7. Never be sorry for yourself or beg sympathy, stop complaining, and actively create the life and job you want.

8. When you do not know something say, "I don't know," and when asked to do something say, "I'll try."

9. Listen carefully when spoken to, ask questions when you do not understand, and do not ask questions about things that do not concern you.

10. Make others feel good when they are around you.

11. Look everyone right in the eye and tell the truth every time.

12. Show up early and sometimes stay late without complaining.

WORKPLACE STATISTICS

Studies show that 4 out of 10 people who change jobs do so because they were subjected to rude, discourteous behavior.

According to a study conducted by Christine Pearson of the University of North Carolina's Kenan-Flager Business School, people who encountered rude behavior from coworkers or supervisors react in the following ways:

22% reduced their productivity intentionally

37% became less committed to
the organization

46% considered a job change

53% spent time worrying about past incidents of rude behavior against them and the possibility of a repeat performance.

Suggested Reading List

Axtell, Roger. <u>Gestures.</u>

Baldridge, Leticia. <u>New Complete Guide to
    Executive Manners.</u>

… <u>The New Manners for the 90s.</u>

Brody, Marjorie. <u>21st Century Pocket Guides
    to Proper Business Protocol</u>
        (4 booklet set):

Booklet 1: <u>Rules for the Wired </u>
Booklet 2: <u>Creating First Impressions—Lasting
    Impressions</u>
Booklet 3: <u>Make the Work Environment Work
    For You</u>
Booklet 4: <u>Have Office, Will Travel: Doing
Business—on the Road</u>

    … <u>21 Common Mistakes for 21st
    Century Business Etiquette.</u>

… <u>Complete Business Etiquette Handbook.</u>

… <u>Professional Impressions: Etiquette For</u>
     <u>Everyone, Every Day.</u>

Dupont, Kay M. <u>Business Etiquette and</u>
     <u>Professionalism.</u>

Fox, Grace. <u>Office Etiquette and Protocol</u>
     <u>(Basics Made Easy).</u>

Garfinkel, Perry, Kaufman, Brian Paul, and the
Editors of Men's Health.
          <u>Command Respect: Cultivate the</u>
          <u>Qualities That Inspire and</u>
          <u>Impress Others.</u>

Kennedy, Lou. <u>Essential Business Etiquette:</u>
          <u>Bottom Line Behavior for Everyday</u>
          <u>Effectiveness.</u>

Klinkenberg, Hilda. <u>At Ease Professionally:</u>
          <u>An Etiquette Guide for the Business</u>
          <u>Arena.</u>

Martin, Judith. <u>Miss Manners' Basic Training:</u>
    <u>Communication.</u>

Sokolosky, Valerie. <u>The Little Instruction</u>
    <u>Book of Business Etiquette: A User</u>
    <u>Friendly, Bite-Sized Guide to Building</u>
    <u>Confidence in the Workplace.</u>

Tuckerman, Nancy & Dunnan, Nancy. <u>The</u>
    <u>Amy Vanderbilt Complete Book of</u>
    <u>Etiquette.</u>

ABOUT THE AUTHOR

Karen S. Hinds, is a keynote speaker, trainer, consultant. Born and raised in the Caribbean island of St. Vincent, Karen combines her knowledge of Caribbean hospitality, British style, and grace to bring a fresh perspective to improving workplace relations. Her presentations are rich with practical lessons drawn from traditional values.

Karen works with organizations to help them develop employees who are professional, polished, and personally effective and with individuals who want to reawaken their spirits.

Based in Boston, Karen is president of The Hinds Company and provides speaking and training services nationally and internationally.

Book Karen for your next speaking engagements, call Toll free: 1-877-902-2775.

Keynotes, Conferences, Seminars, Consulting.

Karen S. Hinds
P. O. Box 260572
Boston, MA 02126
Tel: (617) 296-5242
Toll free 1-877-902-2775
Fax: (617) 296-6786
Visit us online at: www.Karenspeaks.com
Email: Karen@Karenspeaks.com

Order Books:
Fax orders (617) 296-6786
Phone orders toll free: 1-877-902-2775
Order online: www.Karenspeaks.com

Postal Orders:
New Books Publishing
P. O. Box 260572
Boston, MA 02126

YES! YES! YES!

_____**YES!** Please add me to your mailing list so I can learn more about the effects of courtesy in the workplace.

_____**YES!** I want the FREE e-mail subscription to your e-zine "Courtesy Today."

_____ **YES!** I know of a Business/Corporation/ Association that might be interested in on-site training, keynote presentation, or convention breakout. Please call me at the number below.

Name: _________________________________

Phone: _________________________________

Company: _______________________________

Address: ________________________________

Email:__________________________________

Return to: The Hinds Company
              P.O. Box 260572
              Boston, MA 02126
              Fax: 617-296-6786

GIVE THE GIFT OF
Get Along, Get Ahead: 101 Courtesies for the New Workplace
to Your Loved Ones, Friends, and Colleagues

___Yes, I want ___ copies of *Get Along, Get Ahead: 101 Courtesies for the New Workplace* at $14.99 each, plus $3.00 shipping per book. (MA residents please add 5% sales tax.) Foreign orders must be accompanied by money order in US funds. Allow 3-5 days for delivery.

My check or money order for $______is enclosed. Please charge my:

__Visa __MC __Discover __American Express

Name: ____

Organization: ___________________________________

Address: ____

City:__________________________ State: _____ Zip:_________

Phone: ____

Fax: ____

E-mail: ____

Card #:_______________________ Exp Date: ______

Signature: ______________________________________

Please make check payable and return to:

New Books Publishing

P.O. Box 260572

Boston, MA 02126

Call credit card order to: 1-877-902-2775

Fax: 617-296-6786. Email: orders@Karenspeaks.com

GIVE THE GIFT OF
Get Along, Get Ahead: 101 Courtesies for the
New Workplace
to Your Loved Ones, Friends, and Colleagues

___Yes, I want ___ copies of *Get Along, Get Ahead: 101 Courtesies for the New Workplace* at $14.99 each, plus $3.00 shipping per book. (MA residents please add 5% sales tax.) Foreign orders must be accompanied by money order in US funds. Allow 3-5 days for delivery.

My check or money order for $______is enclosed.
Please charge my:
__Visa __MC __Discover __American Express

Name: _______________________________________
Organization: _________________________________
Address: _____________________________________
City:____________________ State: _____ Zip:________
Phone: ______________________________________
Fax: ____
E-mail: ______________________________________
Card #:_____________________ Exp Date: _______
Signature:____________________________________
Please make check payable and return to:
New Books Publishing
P.O. Box 260572
Boston, MA 02126

Call credit card order to: 1-877-902-2775
Fax: 617-296-6786. Email: orders@Karenspeaks.com

NOTES

NOTES